## Dedication

*This devotional is dedicated to my husband, Pastor Zilvan G. Martin; my children: Sarah, Thaddeus, Esther, Earl, Abigail, and Antwan; my grandchildren: Elizabeth, Joanna, Grace, Phebe, ROSE, Esther, Joshua, Elijah, Martin, Devorah, Paige, and Eleanor; and my goddaughter, Desiree.*

*I also dedicate this book to my wonderful parents - the great evangelist, Charles E Lewis, and the mighty PRAYER warrior evangelist, Lottie M. Lewis.*

## Table of Contents

| | |
|---|---|
| Day 1 | 1 |
| Day 2 | 2 |
| Day 3 | 3 |
| Day 4 | 4 |
| Day 5 | 5 |
| Day 6 | 6 |
| Day 7 | 7 |
| Day 8 | 8 |
| Day 9 | 9 |
| Day 10 | 10 |
| Day 11 | 11 |
| Day 12 | 12 |
| Day 13 | 13 |
| Day 14 | 14 |
| Day 15 | 15 |
| Day 16 | 16 |
| Day 17 | 17 |
| Day 18 | 18 |
| Day 19 | 19 |
| Day 20 | 20 |
| Day 21 | 21 |
| Day 22 | 22 |
| Day 23 | 23 |
| Day 24 | 24 |
| Day 25 | 25 |
| Day 26 | 26 |
| Day 27 | 27 |
| Day 28 | 28 |
| Day 29 | 29 |
| Day 30 | 30 |
| Day 31 | 31 |

| | |
|---|---|
| Day 32 | 32 |
| Day 33 | 33 |
| Day 34 | 34 |
| Day 35 | 35 |
| Day 36 | 36 |
| Day 37 | 37 |
| Day 38 | 38 |
| Day 39 | 39 |
| Day 40 | 40 |
| Day 41 | 41 |
| Day 42 | 42 |
| Day 43 | 43 |
| Day 44 | 44 |
| Day 45 | 45 |
| Day 46 | 46 |
| Day 47 | 47 |
| Day 48 | 48 |
| Day 49 | 49 |
| Day 50 | 50 |
| Day 51 | 51 |
| Day 52 | 52 |
| Day 53 | 53 |
| Day 54 | 54 |
| Day 55 | 55 |
| Day 56 | 56 |
| Day 57 | 57 |
| Day 58 | 58 |
| Day 59 | 59 |
| Day 60 | 60 |
| Day 61 | 61 |
| Day 62 | 62 |
| Day 63 | 63 |
| Day 64 | 64 |
| Day 65 | 65 |
| Day 66 | 66 |
| Day 67 | 67 |

| | |
|---|---|
| Day 68 | 68 |
| Day 69 | 69 |
| Day 70 | 70 |
| Day 71 | 71 |
| Day 72 | 72 |
| Day 73 | 73 |
| Day 74 | 74 |
| Day 75 | 75 |
| Day 76 | 76 |
| Day 77 | 77 |
| Day 78 | 78 |
| Day 79 | 79 |
| Day 80 | 80 |
| Day 81 | 81 |
| Day 82 | 82 |
| Day 83 | 83 |
| Day 84 | 84 |
| Day 85 | 85 |
| Day 86 | 86 |
| Day 87 | 87 |
| Day 88 | 88 |
| Day 89 | 89 |
| Day 90 | 90 |
| Day 91 | 91 |
| Day 92 | 92 |
| Day 93 | 93 |
| Day 94 | 94 |
| Day 95 | 95 |
| Day 96 | 96 |
| Day 97 | 97 |
| Day 98 | 98 |
| Day 99 | 99 |
| Day 100 | 100 |

## Day 1

Good morning. GOD is good, and all the time, GOD is good. However, I like to say, "GOD is better than good." He is the best. He is GOD ALMIGHTY, the PRINCE OF PEACE, LORD OF LORDS and KING OF KINGS, The LILY OF THE VALLEY, THE FIRST AND THE LAST, THE BEGINNING AND THE END, Savior, Healer, Keeper. THE LOVE OF MY LIFE. My everything. Oh, sweet wonder, my ticket to HEAVEN.

Everyone have a blessed day and remember you reap what you sow. So be kind, loving, sweet, CHRIST-LIKE. The seed you plant will produce a great harvest. Watch that tongue and attitude. GOD LOVES you, and so do I. Have a wonderful day.

∼

## Day 2

Good morning, everyone. Today is GOD'S day. Let us sow the good attitude seed, let the HOLY GHOST control our tongue so that we can plant only GOD-given seeds. In everyone's life, we meet today, have a blessed day, and remember GOD LOVES you, and so do I.

∼

## Day 3

Good morning, everyone! Today is GOD'S day! Let's show the LOVE of GOD to everyone we meet. Smile, speak kindly, plant some good seeds, watch our attitude, and bite the tongue (let the HOLY GHOST control the tongue). We reap what we sow. Have a blessed day, and remember GOD LOVES you, and so do I.

## Day 4

Good morning, everyone! Today is GOD'S day! Let's plant some good seeds, the seed of truth - not hearsay, gossip, deceit, etc. Be a PEACEMAKER; do not sow seeds of discord. Sow the seed of unconditional LOVE. We must let the HOLY GHOST tame the tongue! Have a blessed day, and remember GOD LOVES you, and so do I.

∽

## Day 5

Good morning, everyone! Today is GOD'S day! It's seed planting time. Let us smile, show LOVE, hug someone, just be plain kind, and think positively. Let us look beyond the faults and see the need of others. Then plant that good seed (speak life into them) and water them, so we all can grow (you know how when you water flowers, and some of the water gets on you!) Have a blessed day, and remember GOD LOVES you, and so do I.

## Day 6

Good morning, everyone! Today is GOD'S day! It's seed planting time. Let's double up on the seeds today. Let's be a tree of life today. Let us be CHRIST-LIKE today so that the fruit on our tree will bless everyone we meet. Just think how many seeds we will be planting when someone eats just one fruit of our tree (all the good seeds inside that fruit, LOVE, JOY, HOPE, PEACE, KINDNESS , and a will to live, etc.). Have a blessed day, and remember GOD LOVES you, and so do I.

## Day 7

Good morning, everyone! Today is GOD'S day! Seedtime and harvest! Today it may seem like we do not have any seed left. We are drained. It's harvest time (reaping time). Eat! Eat! Eat the WORD. Do not eat all your harvest. Save some for planting. I know that your fruit tastes good. Share your harvest so that your next harvest will be even bigger! Have a blessed day, and remember GOD LOVES you, and so do I.

∽

## Day 8

Good morning, everyone! Today is GOD'S day! Sowing and reaping! Seed planting time and harvest! Let us enjoy the harvest today, but remember to save the best of the harvest for sowing. Share cheerfully. Let everyone see JESUS in us today (LOVE, KINDNESS, COMPASSION, FORGIVENESS, etc.). Have a blessed day, and remember GOD LOVES you, and so do I.

## Day 9

Good morning, everyone! Today is GOD'S day! Let's plant seeds today! Start at home! Sow them! Water seeds that others have planted. Let us work this farm together and let GOD ALMIGHTY get the GLORY. HALLELUJAH to the LAMB OF GOD and PRAISE His name, JESUS - THE GREAT I AM. I feel like dancing and shouting! Have a blessed day, and remember GOD LOVES you, and so do I.

∽

## Day 10

Good morning, everyone! Today is GOD'S day! Let us rejoice and be glad - for this starts a new week. So, get replenished while we enjoy the great harvest and plant some more seeds. It is amazing how we enjoy harvest while planting seeds of LOVE, JOY, PEACE, KINDNESS, life, health, finance, etc. GOD is good, and all the time, GOD is good, but I like to say, He is the best, better than good! Have a blessed day, and remember GOD LOVES you, and so do I.

∼

## Day 11

Good morning, everyone! Today is GOD'S day! It is time to plant seeds! Let us let GOD spread His LOVE through us today to everyone we meet!! A little sleepy this morning? Let's give GOD some PRAISE and GLORY. Thank you, JESUS - HALLELUJAH to the LAMB OF GOD. He is our all and all. LORD prepare the hearts (ground) of the people to receive these seeds we are about to plant in JESUS's name, and the church said AMEN. Have a blessed day, and remember GOD LOVES you, and so do I.

∽

## Day 12

Good morning, everyone! Today is GOD'S day! Let us get busy doing the will of our LORD! Seed time and harvest! Planting and reaping! Pray for the PEACE of Jerusalem, PRAY for America, please, the whole world, each other, PRAY for our leaders that watch for our souls. Have a blessed day, and remember GOD LOVES you, and so do I.

∼

## Day 13

*G*ood morning, everyone! Today is GOD'S day! The sowers and the reaper! Today we can be either sowers or reapers! Do not get upset with the reapers because they reap where they have not sowed. We all must rejoice together. Let us wait patiently for our turn. GOD knows when we should be the reaper. If too soon, we might eat all the harvest and not save any for planting (if there is no seed to plant, what happens? Think about it). It all belongs to GOD, not us. Read John 4:34-39. Have a blessed day, and remember that GOD LOVES you, and so do I.

## Day 14

Good morning, everyone! Today is GOD'S day! Let us rejoice and be glad in it. Seed planting time and harvest! Let's continue to plant great seeds of RIGHTEOUSNESS! Let us labor today. Water the seeds and do not worry about the tares; leave them to GOD ALMIGHTY! Just work. JESUS said in Luke 10:2 (KJV), "Therefore said He unto them, the harvest truly is great, but the labourers are few: PRAY ye, therefore, the LORD of the harvest, that He would send forth labourers into His harvest." The labor is hard work but let us be consistent; there is a reward! Have a blessed day, and remember GOD LOVES you, and so do I.

∼

## Day 15

Good morning, everyone! Today is GOD'S day! Let us plant some pedigree seeds today so our harvest will look just like our master (JESUS). Today remember GOD'S WORD said in Psalms 34:18-19 says, "The LORD is nigh unto them that are of a broken heart; and saveth such as be of a contrite SPIRIT. Many are the afflictions of the righteous: but the LORD delivereth Him out of them all." Have a blessed day, and remember GOD LOVES you, and so do I.

∼

## Day 16

Good morning, everyone! Today is GOD'S day! Let us rejoice and be glad in it. Let's sow seeds today. The kind of seeds that we would LOVE to reap. Psalms 30:5 (KJV) says, "For His anger endureth but a moment; in His favor is life: weeping may endure for a night, but JOY cometh in the morning." Let us be patient. Luke 21:19 (KJV) states, "In your patience possess ye your souls." Have a blessed day, and remember GOD LOVES you, and so do I.

∼

## Day 17

Good morning, everyone! Today is GOD'S day! Let us spread the WORD (the Gospel of JESUS CHRIST); it is HEAVEN or HELL. JESUS is the only way! The Bible said in John 14:5-6 (KJV) says, "Thomas saith unto him, LORD, we know not whither thou goest; and how can we know the way? JESUS saith unto him, I am the way, the truth, and the life: no man cometh unto the father, but by me." It's JESUS' way or no way! We who know the way must spread it plant pedigree seeds everywhere. It is a command! Let us live it, for our lives are our greatest witness! Have a blessed day, and remember GOD LOVES you, and so do I.

## Day 18

Good morning, everyone! Today is GOD'S day! It's time to let JESUS shine so bright in us that the world sees JESUS instead of us when they look at us, pass by us, talk to us, bump into us, steal from us, etc. We have to plant seeds of RIGHTEOUSNESS. The world needs us to sow JESUS into their lives. Believe it or not, the world is crying for help (like a baby crying for its mother). So today, let's watch our attitude, be thankful, appreciative, and BE RESPECTFUL of our GOD! Have a blessed day, and remember that GOD LOVES you, and so do I.

∼

## Day 19

Good morning, everyone! Today is GOD'S day! Another day to plant JESUS' seeds into the lives of everyone we meet, direct or indirectly (for there are people who we pass or pass us accidentally who need a good morning or just a smile). Let us not get too busy that our attitude is not showing JESUS. JESUS took time with the outcast, the children, the downtrodden, etc. Be kind to the one that may never be able to give you anything in return, for we are not working for ourselves, but we are working for the KING OF KINGS and LORD OF LORDS, JESUS CHRIST! Have a blessed day, and remember GOD LOVES you, and so do I.

~

## Day 20

Good morning, everyone! Today is GOD'S day! Seed planting time! Let us plant fields of righteous seeds! Spread the LOVE of GOD around! Speak into the lives of everyone you meet! GOD'S WORD said in John 14:14 (KJV), "If ye shall ask anything in my name, I will do it." So, let's start asking for whole schools, towns, homes; our GOD can do anything but fail. Have a blessed day, and remember GOD LOVES you, and so do I.

∼

## Day 21

Good morning, everyone! Today is GOD'S day! Time to plant some more Godly seeds for the kingdom of GOD. Just think. Someone plants a seed in our lives at a random time. Did that seed come up right away, or did it take some time? So let us be patient as we plant seeds. Let us ask GOD to prepare the hearts of the people to accept the WORD of GOD! James 1:4 (KJV) says, "But let patience have her perfect work, that ye may be perfect and entire, wanting nothing." That patient blesses us. Keep planting. Have a blessed day, and remember GOD LOVES you, and so do I.

## Day 22

Good morning, everyone! Today is GOD'S day! Let us water some seed that someone else has planted while someone is watering some seeds we planted. We are in this together. Let us work wholeheartedly for the kingdom of GOD, for that's all that matters (that GOD gets the GLORY). One plants, another waters, but it's GOD that gives the increase. Thank you, JESUS. So plant some Godly seed and water some Godly plants today. Have a blessed day, and remember GOD LOVES you, and so do I.

∼

## Day 23

Good morning! Today is GOD'S day! Let us rejoice in it and be glad in it, for great is the LORD and greatly to be PRAISEd! Hold on, seed planters. Harvest is coming! Look, the fields are already white, ready for laborers. Now let us be good laborers for the wages are great, and they carry supernatural and natural benefits. I know you might be tired, but press on, as the old saints would say. It will soon be crowning day. We must not give up. We are too close! Have a blessed day, and remember GOD LOVES you, and so do I.

## Day 24

Good morning, everyone! Today is GOD'S day! Let us show the world who we serve, the KING OF KINGS, the LORD OF LORDS, the only ALMIGHTY GOD, the PRINCE OF PEACE, JESUS, the one and only true and LIVING GOD. Let us do some Godly seed planting today. Let's have the smell of JESUS on us, that sweet smell that people want to know where you brought that. It's free, you say! It's free! Let me tell you! Have a blessed day, and remember GOD LOVES you, and so do I.

～

## Day 25

Good morning, everyone! Today is GOD'S day! Still seed planting time! Let us plant some LOVE in someone's life today, and it will brighten our day as well. Remember, we cannot brighten someone else's day and ours not be brightened. We reap what we sow! Let us do it today! Have a blessed day, and remember GOD LOVES you, and so do I.

∾

## Day 26

Good morning, everyone! Today is GOD'S day! Time to go to work in the LORD's vineyard! Matthew 20:6b-7 (KJV) says, "Why stand ye here all the day idle? They say unto him, because no man hath hired us. He saith unto them, go ye also into the vineyard; and whatsoever is right, that shall ye receive." Let us work faithfully, for GOD is our boss, and He will pay us, and what we get will be right. His records are perfect! Be happy with your pay. Little or much, it's right. Smile. We know our works. No work, no pay! It's not how long, but the quality of the work, no matter how small the task! Have a blessed day, and remember GOD LOVES you, and so do I.

∼

## Day 27

Good morning, everyone! Today is GOD'S day! Let us plant the seed of life in someone today, JESUS. Give them JESUS! By our actions, attitude, smiles, KINDNESS, JOY, patience, LOVE, and PEACE. Now watch the showers of blessing that fall on us in return. Thank you, JESUS! Have a blessed day, and remember GOD LOVES you, and so do I.

∽

Day 28
_____

Good morning, everyone! Today is GOD'S day! Let us plant some Godly seeds today. As we plant seeds, we are blessing others and ourselves, for there will be a harvest. Keep working for GOD. GOD sees our labor of LOVE, and He will reward us! Smile! Have a blessed day, and remember GOD LOVES you, and so do I.

## Day 29

Good morning, everyone! Today is GOD'S day! Let us speak life into some hurting people today! Proverbs 18:21 (KJV) says, "Death and life are in the power of the tongue: and they that LOVE it shall eat the fruit thereof." Have a blessed day, and remember GOD LOVES you, and so do I.

∾

## Day 30

Good morning, everyone! Today is GOD'S day! Let us lift up the name of JESUS, our soon coming KING! In addition, plant some seeds of GRACE today, as GOD ALMIGHTY shines on us. In whatever state we are in, let's PRAISE him. 1 Timothy 6:6 (KJV) says, "But GODLINESS with contentment is great gain." Have a blessed day, and remember GOD LOVES you, and so do I.

~

## Day 31

Good morning, everyone! Today is GOD'S day! Let us rejoice and be glad in it. Let us plant some seeds of PEACE. Matthew 5:9 (KJV) says, "Blessed are the PEACEMAKERS: for they shall be called the children of GOD." We are blessed when we are PEACEMAKERS. Wow! What a wonderful GOD we serve. JESUS is the PRINCE OF PEACE! Have a blessed day, and remember GOD LOVES you, and so do I.

∽

## Day 32

Good morning, everyone! Today is GOD'S day! Let's keep up the good work planting those Godly seeds. It might seem like the weeds (tares) are growing faster than your Godly seeds, but do not worry, just keep planting Godly seeds. GOD got this. Be patient. Luke 21:19 (KJV) says, "In your patience possess ye your souls." Have a blessed day, and remember GOD LOVES you, and so do I.

~

## Day 33

Good morning, everyone! Today is GOD'S day! Let's keep working in the vineyard of the LORD! For He will not forget our labor of LOVE. Hebrews 6:10 (KJV) says, "For GOD is not unrighteous to forget your work and labour of LOVE, which ye have shewed toward His name, in that, ye have ministered to the saints, and do minister." So, smile and plant some more seeds of RIGHTEOUSNESS into someone's life today! Have a blessed day, and remember GOD LOVES you, and so do I.

## Day 34

Good morning, everyone! Today is GOD'S day! Let's plant seeds of MERCY today! For we have a GOD who is very merciful to us. Lamentations 3:21-23 (KJV) says, "This I recall to my mind, therefore have I HOPE. It is of the LORD's mercies that we are not consumed, because His COMPASSIONS fail not. They are new every morning: great is thy faithfulness." Have blessed day, and remember GOD LOVES you, and so do I.

∼

## Day 35

Good morning, everyone! Today is GOD'S day! Let's bless ourselves by blessing someone else, for we cannot bless someone else without it be a blessing to us. Plant seeds of JOY, PEACE, LOVE, KINDNESS, etc. Have blessed day, and remember GOD LOVES you, and so do I.

∼

## Day 36

Good morning, everyone! Today is GOD'S day! Let's rejoice and be glad in it. Smile and think of the SONg that says when I think of the GOODNESS of JESUS and all that He has done for me (us), my (our) soul cries out HALLELUJAH, I (we) thank GOD for saving me (us). Feed someone the bread of life today. Fill my cup LORD and let it overflow. Let it soak those around us. Have a blessed day, and remember GOD LOVES you, and so do I.

∼

## Day 37

Good morning, everybody! Today is GOD'S day! Let us continue to be faithful to ALMIGHTY GOD and plant seeds of JOY, PEACE, LOVE, and PRAYER. We, the children of GOD, have the answer to our needs and the world (JESUS, the ALMIGHTY GOD). Have a blessed day, and remember GOD LOVES you, and so do I.

## Day 38

Good morning, everyone! Today is GOD'S day! Let us be thankful, PRAISE GOD, and WORSHIP Him for who He is (GOD ALMIGHTY, the PRINCE OF PEACE, KING OF KINGS, and LORD OF LORDS. He is our LORD). Plant those Godly seeds today. Have a blessed day, and remember GOD LOVES you, and so do I.

∽

## Day 39

Good morning, everyone! Today is GOD'S day! Singing, He is sweet. I know dark clouds can rise and stormy winds can blow, but I'll tell the world wherever I go that I found a savior, and he's sweet, I know. Let's plant those seeds today so that the world will know that He's sweet and that we are His children. Plant, plant, and plant. Have a blessed day, and remember GOD LOVES you, and so do I.

~

## Day 40

Good morning, everyone! Today is GOD'S day! The blessing of the LORD be upon us. Thank GOD for His amazing GRACE. For it is by His GRACE that we are what we are in Him. Let's PRAISE and WORSHIP Him. For He alone is WORTHY. Seed planting and harvest time; let's plant those seeds of RIGHTEOUSNESS. Smile! Have a blessed day, and remember GOD LOVES you, and so do I.

∼

## Day 41

Good morning, everyone! Today is GOD'S day! Thank GOD for GOD giving His SON as a sacrifice for us while yet in our sin seeds and sinful acts. Today, as we plant seeds of RIGHTEOUSNESS, let us really pounder in our hearts what JESUS did for us (undeserving sinner). The suffering, the humiliation in the eyes of others. And His father turning His head from Him because of the sins (the cup) He bore in His body for us. Smile, for we have something to rejoice about (that great sacrifice, that unconditional LOVE for us). Have a blessed day, and remember GOD LOVES you, and so do I.

∼

## Day 42

Good morning, everyone! Today is GOD'S day! Let us rejoice today knowing that we have a savior who willing gave up His life for us (undeserving people) to have eternal life and live with Him forever. That's a LOVE that cannot be matched ( unconditional LOVE). PRAISE be to our GOD who sent His SON, HALLELUJAH to the LAMB OF GOD, GLORY to GOD in the highest, thank GOD for salvation through His SON, JESUS - tears of JOY. Have a blessed day, and remember GOD LOVES you, and so do I.

~

## Day 43

Good morning, everyone! Today is GOD'S day! PRAISE be to our GOD who sent His SON to die for our sins so that we could live with Him forever. Thank GOD JESUS ROSE that third day. Just like He said He would. Today plant lots of righteous seeds, for there are many who have not excepted or know Him (JESUS) as their personal SAVOIR! Have a blessed day, and remember GOD LOVES you, and so do I.

∽

Day 44
---

Good morning, everyone! Today is GOD'S day! Let's plant an abundance of HOLY seeds today. For we need them, and the world around us needs to see us doing the will of our LORD and Savior, JESUS CHRIST. LORD, help us today as we carry out your will with JOY, for the JOY of the LORD is our strength. Have a blessed day, and remember GOD LOVES you, and so do I.

∼

## Day 45

Good morning, everyone! Today is GOD'S day! Let's PRAISE him! Let's sing aloud unto the LORD our GOD, our deliverer, our keeper, our way MAKER, our sanctifier, our everything! PRAISE be to our GOD who has redeemed our lives from destruction! HALLELUJAH, GLORY, what a wonder He (JESUS) is. Do not forget to plant those seeds that GOD has planted in us. Have a blessed day, and remember GOD LOVES you, and so do I.

∽

## Day 46

Good morning, everyone! Today is GOD'S day! Surprise! GOD LOVES us more than we can imagine! He wants to do us good. So, smile! He LOVES us with unconditional LOVE. How sweet it is to know that GOD LOVES us like that. So let us get going and plant some seeds (Godly seeds) today. Have a blessed day, and remember GOD LOVES you, and so do I.

∼

## Day 47

Good morning, everyone! Today is GOD'S day! Let us PRAY for a mighty harvest as we plant seeds of RIGHTEOUSNESS in good ground. Pray for the guidance of the LORD, and put our all into the work of the LORD, for it will be a great blessing to us and our seed. Psalms 103:1 (KJV) states, "Bless the LORD, o my soul: and all that is within me, bless His Holy name." Give Him PRAISE and WORSHIP His mighty name. Have a blessed day, and remember GOD LOVES you, and so do I.

∽

## Day 48

Good morning, everyone! Today is GOD'S day! Smile. Today is your GOD'S day. Rejoice and be glad in it, and sing songs of PRAISE to him. This morning bless yourselves by praising him, feeling the showers, getting soaked, as a child who LOVES to play in the rain. Let His showers soak you to the marrow of the bone (the innermost part of the soul). Have a blessed day, and remember that GOD LOVES you, and so do I.

## Day 49

Good morning, everyone! Today is GOD'S day! Let's continue to work, planting seeds of RIGHTEOUSNESS. There are plenty who need food. Smile and be happy our GOD is in control. Shout HALLELUJAH, our GOD reigns. Isaiah 54:17 (KJV) says, "No weapon that is formed against thee shall prosper; and every tongue that shall rise against thee in judgment thou shalt condemn. This is the heritage of the servants of the LORD, and their RIGHTEOUSNESS is of me, saith the LORD." Have a blessed day, and remember GOD LOVES you, and so do I.

∼

## Day 50

Good morning, everyone! Today is GOD'S day! Thank you, JESUS, for another day to share your precious fruit. Galatians 5:22-23 (KJV) states, "But the fruit of the SPIRIT is LOVE, JOY, PEACE, LONGSUFFERING, GENTLENESS, GOODNESS , FAITH, MEEKNESS, TEMPERANCE: against such there is no law. Let's spread it around, our life is our greatest witness." Have a blessed day, and remember GOD LOVES you, and so do I.

∼

## Day 51

Good morning, everyone! Today is GOD'S day! Let's sing PRAISEs to the LORD of our salvation! For He alone is WORTHY of PRAISES and GLORY! Let's bow down before Him in true WORSHIP by planting all those seeds that He has planted in us by the HOLY GHOST! It's raining, raining, raining, and there is a blessing in the rain! Let us soak it up. Smile. Have a blessed day, and remember GOD LOVES you, and so do I.

∽

## Day 52

Good morning, everyone! Today is GOD'S day! Let's plant some HEAVENLY seeds today - seeds of JOY, LOVE, PEACE, KINDNESS, GENTLENESS, the Gospel of JESUS CHRIST. Let us let our passion for JESUS overflow today and brighten up our surroundings. HALLELUJAH, GLORY, He's WORTHY. PRAY, PRAY! Have a blessed day, and remember GOD LOVES you, and so do I.

∽

## Day 53

Good morning, everyone! Today is GOD'S day! Let us go forth praising ALMIGHTY GOD. Who only is WORTHY of all the GLORY and PRAISE, smile for VICTORY is our, through our LORD JESUS CHRIST. Plant those seeds that JESUS has given us, and He will give the increase. Plant everywhere we go. Let's be positive, for we serve the ALL-POWERFUL GOD! The ALL-KNOWING GOD! EVERYWHERE at the same time GOD. Thank GOD for JESUS. Have a blessed day, and remember GOD LOVES you, and so do I.

∼

## Day 54

Good morning, everyone! Today is GOD'S day! Thank GOD for another day to PRAISE and WORSHIP him. In the beauty of HOLINESS. Plant seeds of RIGHTEOUSNESS. Let us give some JOY to the people we meet today. For GOD is good. Better yet, He is the best. HALLELUJAH, GLORY to GOD. Have a blessed day, and remember GOD LOVES you, and so do I.

∼

## Day 55

Good morning, everyone! Today is GOD'S day! Let's sow seeds of PEACE today. Matthew 5:9 (KJV) states, "Blessed are the PEACEMAKERS: for they shall be called the children of GOD." PEACE brings JOY, calm to the storm. Let's share that PEACE everywhere we go today, no matter the problem. Keep calm. JESUS got this or that. Have a blessed day, and remember GOD LOVES you, and so do I.

∽

## Day 56

Good morning, everyone! Today is GOD'S day! Let us shout to the LORD, for He has done marvelous things for us! Seed planting and harvest time. Whether you are planting or harvesting, you are being blessed. So, let's shout to the KING OF KINGS, JESUS, our soon coming Savior, for VICTORY is ours. Do we hear the JOY-bells ringing in our souls? Have a blessed day, and remember GOD LOVES you, and so do I.

∾

## Day 57

Good morning, everyone! Today is GOD'S day! Time to shout HALLELUJAH to the ALMIGHTY GOD! We must PRAISE Him no matter what our problem is, for there is deliverance in our PRAISE. The JOY of the LORD is our strength. Let's plant those righteous seeds today. Smile! Have a blessed day, and remember GOD LOVES you, and so do I.

∼

## Day 58

Good morning, everyone! Today is GOD'S day! Let us honor our king (JESUS), crying HOLY, HOLY, HOLY is the LORD our GOD! For HOLY and reverence is His name. Plant those righteous seeds today and labor in the vineyard, for there are hearts already ripe ready for picking. Let us shake ourselves and get busy. Smile! Have a blessed day, and remember GOD LOVES you, and so do I.

∽

## Day 59

Good morning, everyone! Today is GOD'S day! Let's walk in the VICTORY that JESUS has already won for us and plant HOLY seeds today. Smile! JESUS LOVES us and wants what's best for us! So spread some SONSHINE (JESUS) today. I promise it will brighten your day and those around you. Have a blessed day. Remember, GOD LOVES you, and so do I.

∼

## Day 60

Good morning, everyone! Today is GOD'S day! Let us rejoice and be glad, sing PRAISEs, shout for JOY, for He alone is WORTHY, and let us bow down and WORSHIP him. Let us sow seeds of RIGHTEOUSNESS everywhere we go today. Have a blessed day, and remember GOD LOVES you, and so do I.

## Day 61

Good morning, everyone! Today is GOD'S day! Let us bless His HOLY name! Leap for JOY today, run for PEACE, and skip for LOVE. Now dance and shout to the LORD, for today we have the VICTORY (in CHRIST JESUS). Have a blessed day, and remember GOD LOVES you, and so do I.

∽

## Day 62

Good morning, everyone! Today is GOD'S day! Time to shine brighter than the noonday sun because the SON (JESUS) is in us. HALLELUJAH, GLORY HALLELUJAH, ALMIGHTY GOD, THE GREAT I AM THAT I AM. What a wonder He is. JESUS is our provider, our deliverer, our keeper, our Savior, our everything. VICTORY today is ours. Have a blessed day, and remember GOD LOVES you, and so do I.

## Day 63

Good morning, everyone! Today is GOD'S day! Let us plant seeds of FAITH, believing that GOD has open the hearts of people waiting for us to share His word (JESUS) with. Let us not miss them, thinking they do not look ready or like they don't want to be bothered. Leave it to the ALMIGHTY GOD. Let us be JOYFUL and shine brighter than the noonday sun and knock them off their beast, for we have the SON (JESUS) in us. Have a blessed day, and remember GOD LOVES you, and so do I.

∽

## Day 64

Good morning, everyone! Today is GOD'S day! Plant, plant, and plant those righteous seeds. For we are to work until the day is done, keep our relationship with our LORD nourished, and in good standing, for the times are critical. Smile and shout loud to our GOD for JOY, for the JOY of the LORD is our strength. Have a blessed day, and remember GOD LOVES you, and so do I.

~

## Day 65

Good morning, everyone! Today is GOD'S day! Time to sow seeds of LOVE. For GOD is LOVE. So let us spread that Godly LOVE around today. Thank GOD that His LOVE is unconditional. So, let's remember that today as we spread GOD'S LOVE that's in us. Have a blessed day, and remember GOD LOVES you, and so do I.

∼

## Day 66

Good morning, everyone! Today is GOD'S day! The start of a new beginning. Come on and bless the LORD with me, and let us shout with the voice of triumphant, for the LORD has given us the cities (VICTORY). VICTORY is ours. Thanks be to our GOD who reigns for all eternity! Plant those righteous seeds today and watch GOD work. Have a blessed day, and remember GOD LOVES you, and so do I.

## Day 67

Good morning, everyone! Today is GOD'S day! Let us PRAISE our MAKER for all His wonderful acts to us this glorious morning. Let us sing aloud of His GOODNESS , for He (JESUS) is the best! Sow some seeds of PEACE today. Matthew 5:9 (KJV) says, "Blessed are the PEACEMAKERS: for they shall be called the children of GOD." We all need the PEACE of GOD. Oh, to know His PEACE is sweet. Have a blessed day, and remember GOD LOVES you, and so do I.

∾

## Day 68

Good morning, everyone! Today is GOD'S day! Let's be thankful and plant seeds of JOY, LOVE, GENTLENESS, PEACE, etc. Plant righteous seeds, and watch how we grow. Let it rain down slowly and saturate our body (soul and SPIRIT) from the inside out. Let our cup overflow, and bless all those around us. Feel the rain, shout HALLELUJAH, GLORY to the LAMB OF GOD, He is WORTHY. Have a blessed day, and remember GOD LOVES you, and so do I.

∼

## Day 69

Good morning, everyone! Today is GOD'S day! Let us PRAISE GOD for His GOODNESS , MERCY, and GRACE that He lavishes on us every day. So let us plant some on the people we meet today with a smile that says JESUS LOVES you unconditionally. Show some COMPASSION and thank GOD for His MERCY! Lamentations 3:22-23 (KJV) says, "It is of the LORD's mercies that we are not consumed because His COMPASSIONS fail not. They are new every morning: great is thy faithfulness." Have a blessed day, and remember GOD LOVES you, and so do I.

∽

## Day 70

Good morning, everyone! Today is GOD'S day! Let us rejoice and be glad that our GOD is in control! Let us be thankful and give Him PRAISE for He is WORTHY, shout HALLELUJAH, shout GLORY, shout thank you, JESUS, for we are more than conquerors! Romans 8:37 (KJV) says, "Nay, in all these things we are more than conquerors through Him that loved us." He (JESUS) LOVES us unconditionally. Have a blessed day, and remember GOD LOVES you, and so do I.

## Day 71

Good morning, everyone! Today is GOD'S day! Let us PRAY, PRAY, and PRAY! PRAY, lifting up HOLY hands. Prayer is the weapon of warfare. Pray and not faint, for we need to spread those righteous seeds today as never before, for the PRAYER of the righteous carries great weight! James 5:16b (KJV) says, "The effectual fervent PRAYER of a righteous man availeth much." Let us use the weapon of warfare to the fullest extent, HALLELUJAH. Have a blessed day, and remember GOD LOVES you, and so do I.

∽

## Day 72

Good morning, everyone! Today is GOD'S day! Let us be a blessing to someone today and watch GOD be a blessing to us. GLORY! We cannot bless someone else and not get blessed, too, for we will surely reap what we sow. So plant seeds of RIGHTEOUSNESS. GOD can not lie. Galatians 6:7 (KJV) says, "Be not deceived; GOD is not mocked: for whatsoever a man soweth, that shall He also reap." Let us sow spiritual and natural seeds. My GOD!. Have a blessed day, and remember GOD LOVES you, and so do I.

## Day 73

Good morning, everyone! Today is GOD'S day! Smile and say GLORY to the KING OF KINGS and LORD OF LORDS, for He is WORTHY. Let us be thankful for all His GRACE and MERCY that He has bestowed upon us. Let us share that GRACE and MERCY freely today, for we all were undeserving, but our ALMIGHTY GOD lavished it on us. Thank you, JESUS, GLORY! What a wonder He is! HALLELUJAH to the LAMB OF GOD! Have a blessed day, and remember GOD LOVES you, and so do I.

## Day 74

Good morning, everyone! Today is GOD'S day! It's HOLINESS or HELL. It's right or wrong. Let us show the world who JESUS is by sowing Godly seeds today that penetrate the soul of man. Holiness is our life. Thank GOD for the HOLY GHOST (SPIRIT). Let's walk in VICTORY today, for the battle is the LORD's. Let us leap for JOY. GLORY! GLORY! HALLELUJAH! Thank you, JESUS! THE GREAT I AM THAT I AM! Have a blessed day, and remember GOD LOVES you, and so do I.

∼

## Day 75

Good morning, everyone! Today is GOD'S day! Let's PRAISE Him for the rain, showers of rain, let it soak us through and through. Let us look through the eyes of FAITH, seeing all the souls running to the kingdom of GOD. Let us, with open arms, cleave to them and, with our overflow, soak them until they are rooted and grounded in the WORD! Let us sacrifice all our means for souls, for we were once one of them, and someone sacrificed their means for us. Have a blessed day, and remember GOD LOVES you, and so do I.

∽

## Day 76

Good morning, everyone! Today is GOD'S day! Let's PRAY for a mighty harvest, for we all have loved ones who can be part of that harvest. Let's fish in the deep waters where there are schools of fish. And let us run through the schools of fish spreading seeds of RIGHTEOUSNESS. Thank GOD for JESUS, who has given us a lively HOPE. A HOPE that will not fade away. GLORY HALLELUJAH! PEACE and JOY in the HOLY GHOST. Have a blessed day, and remember GOD LOVES you, and so do I.

## Day 77

Good morning, everyone! Today is GOD'S day! Let us WORSHIP the LORD, our GOD, with a shout of thunderous PRAISE, for He is WORTHY. Don't forget to sow seeds of RIGHTEOUSNESS today. Let us lift Him in the beauty of HOLINESS. For He (JESUS) is HOLY, sing unto the LORD a new song, bow down before Him - run, jump. Skip, leap and dance before our king like David did (if you cannot do it naturally, do it in your SPIRIT). Have a blessed day, and remember GOD LOVES you, and so do I.

∽

## Day 78

Good morning, everyone! Today is GOD'S day! Let us rejoice and be glad in it. Plant seeds of JOY, the JOY of the LORD is our strength. Let's flex some muscles today, for the LORD gives liberally to the souls that ask. You need JOY, PEACE, FAITH, the HOLY GHOST (SPIRIT) gives them at no charge! They are free. Smile! No money is required. Just ask. Thank you, JESUS. HALLELUJAH. Let's give Him (JESUS) a thunderous shout of PRAISE. Let's wake up those that are asleep. My GOD, what a wonder He is. There is no GOD like our GOD. He is the only true and LIVING GOD. Have a blessed day, and remember GOD LOVES you, and so do I.

## Day 79

Good morning, everyone! Today is GOD'S day! Let us sing aloud to our MAKER , for He is WORTHY (JESUS) He is the everlasting king, shout GLORY, ALMIGHTY GOD, PRINCE OF PEACE, ROSE OF SHARON, LILY OF THE VALLEY, my what a GOD we serve. Let's be about His business today, planting seeds of HOPE and LOVE. Have a blessed day, and remember GOD LOVES you, and so do I.

∼

## Day 80

Good morning, everyone! Today is GOD'S day! Let us give true WORSHIP to our ALMIGHTY GOD! For it is by His GRACE that we are here this morning! Smile, laugh, and be thankful that the ALMIGHTY has blessed us with His GRACE. Let us plant seeds of GRACE and MERCY today. For it is by His GRACE and MERCY that we are here. Give Him some thunderous PRAISE - run, jump, wave your hands in the air, and shout HALLELUJAH to the LAMB OF GOD (JESUS). Have a blessed day, and remember GOD LOVES you, and so do I.

## Day 81

Good morning, everyone! Today is GOD'S day! Let us rejoice and be glad, for great is the LORD and greatly to be PRAISED! Let's sow seeds of RIGHTEOUSNESS today. Spread the word of the LORD all around. Let that LIVING WATER that's springing up in us overflow all over the places we go, and bless everyone we pass today! Smile, we have the VICTORY in JESUS. Have a blessed day, and remember GOD LOVES you, and so do I.

## Day 82

Good morning, everyone! Today is GOD'S day! Let's be thankful for His GRACE and MERCY! Let us dig way down in our soul, heart, mind, and body and give Him (JESUS) a thunderous shout of PRAISE and WORSHIP that shakes the earth and scatter our seeds of MERCY everywhere this morning and throughout the day! Pray for a mighty move of GOD as we go about our daily chores. Have a blessed day, and remember GOD LOVES you, and so do I.

∾

## Day 83

Good morning, everyone! Today is GOD'S day! Let us plant, plant, and plant Godly seeds today, for the harvest is plenteous. Let's show them (the world) who the real JESUS is by our LOVE for him, spread that unconditional LOVE all over until the meanest soul smiles! We can do it through the power of JESUS that works in us. Let our lives be a witness to the world. Beat them with LOVE. Have a blessed day, and remember GOD LOVES you, and so do I.

∽

## Day 84

Good morning, everyone! Today is GOD'S day! It's time to show some unconditional LOVE. Unconditional LOVE is a mighty seed that causes people to take note of, to wonder. Even though our enemies don't understand that kind of LOVE, it puzzles them. Let's heap coals of fire on their heads. So, plant that seed of LOVE today for the world needs it, and we do, too. Let us shine brighter than the sun, for we have the SON (JESUS) in us. Have a blessed day, and remember GOD LOVES you, and so do I.

∼

## Day 85

Good morning, everyone! Today is GOD'S day! Shout HALLELUJAH to the LAMB OF GOD, for He alone is WORTHY. Sing aloud unto the ROCK of our salvation JESUS, KING OF KINGS, LORD OF LORDS, the ALMIGHTY GOD, EL SHADDAI, the GOD that's more than enough. Let us let the world know that JESUS is the answer to their (the world's) problems. Spread those HOLY seeds today of LOVE, JOY, PEACE, GENTLENESS, and KINDNESS. Have a blessed day, and remember GOD LOVES you, and so do I.

## Day 86

Good morning, everyone! Today is GOD'S day! Let us be thankful, grateful, and appreciative of our LORD and Savior, JESUS CHRIST, today by our lifestyle and planting seeds of LOVE. Unconditional LOVE, for we are the light of the world. So let our light outshine the bright sunlight. Let's have the world rubbing their eyes, smile! So, let's show them (the world) who JESUS is, the real JESUS. Have a blessed day, and remember GOD LOVES you, and so do I.

∼

## Day 87

Good morning, everyone! Today is GOD'S day! Let's shower our enemies with blessings today. Let's plant some of that JESUS LOVE on them and keep moving, do not stop unless we are invited to stop. Be a live wire, loose on the ground, sparks (LOVE) flying all over the place. The enemies won't know what hit them! Then plant the seed! The Gospel of JESUS CHRIST! What an electrifying day this will be. Have a blessed day, and remember that GOD LOVES you, and so do I.

~

## Day 88

Good morning, everyone! Today is GOD'S day! PRAISE GOD, for He is in control. Nothing can happen without His permission. So, sing aloud of the GOODNESS of JESUS. Shout aloud. He is the king! THE GREAT I AM THAT I AM, the LILY OF THE VALLEY! PRAISE and WORSHIP Him until there is a shaking in the valley that frightens the enemies. Plant, plant, and plant seeds of PRAISE and WORSHIP! Shout HALLELUJAH! Have a blessed day, and remember GOD LOVES you, and so do I.

## Day 89

Good morning, everyone! Today is GOD'S day! Let us rejoice and be glad. For we are in the hands of ALMIGHTY GOD, and no one can pluck us out. HALLELUJAH to the LAMB OF GOD. Let's plants some righteous seeds today - whatever our situation, crises, problem, etc. Today if you do not know what to say, just say JESUS. I am a witness that calling His name works for whatever we need it, in the name of JESUS. Keep planting those Godly seeds. They will come up. Smile! Have a blessed day, and remember GOD LOVES you, and so do I.

## Day 90

Good morning, everyone! Today is GOD'S day! Let us PRAISE our MAKER , the GOD of all gods! For it is good to know who JESUS is, the LILY OF THE VALLEY, the BRIGHT AND MORNING STAR, the CONQUERING LION OF JUDAH, the ALMIGHTY GOD, KING OF KINGS, LORD OF LORDS, THE GREAT I AM THAT I AM! We could go on and on and never finish. So let us plant some HOLY seeds today for the KING that reigns and rules forever, our LORD and Savior, JESUS CHRIST! Do we really understand who we serve, my GOD, what a GOD we serve, no limits, ALL-POWERFUL! ALL-KNOWING! HALLELUJAH! Have a blessed day, and remember GOD LOVES you, and so do I.

∾

## Day 91

Good morning, everyone! Today is GOD'S day! Let's sow some righteous seeds on good ground, ask GOD what good ground to sow on for what we think is good ground may not be good ground. GOD looks at the heart; we look at the outer appearance. Let's trust GOD ALMIGHTY! He is never wrong! Let JESUS sweeten your day, for no enemies can stop us when we walk in the VICTORY that JESUS has already won for us. GLORY! Walk! Walk, shouting JESUS all the way. Have a blessed day, and remember GOD LOVES you, and so do I.

## Day 92

Good morning, everyone! Today is GOD'S day! Let us PRAY, PRAY, and PRAY some more! Our world is in trouble. Let us thank GOD because He gave us the answer! 2 Chronicles 7:14 (KJV) says, "If my people, which are called by my name, shall humble themselves, and PRAY, and seek my face, and turn from their wicked ways; then will I hear from HEAVEN, and will forgive their sin, and will heal their land." GOD'S people have to get it straight! Thank GOD! GLORY! HALLELUJAH! Have a blessed day, and remember GOD LOVES you, and so do I.

∽

## Day 93

Good morning, everyone! Today is GOD'S day! Let's do some shouts of thunderous PRAISE to our GOD, for He is WORTHY. Let's PRAY for the power of the HOLY GHOST (SPIRIT) to saturate and soak us inside and outside! Until the overflow falls on the meanest sinners, and they cannot do anything but say I yield LORD JESUS. We need to do some fasting and praying. Shout HALLELUJAH, GLORY. He's WORTHY. Thank you, JESUS! Let's get the blood heated up in our veins so that the blood of JESUS can boil in us. And we will say like Jeremiah 20:9 (KJV) says, "Then I said, I will not make mention of him, nor speak any more in His name. But His word was in mine heart as a burning fire shut up in my bones, and I was weary with forbearing, and I could not stay." Have a blessed day, and remember GOD LOVES you, and so do I.

## Day 94

Good morning, everyone! Today is GOD'S day! Let us sing aloud of His GOODNESS, JOY, GENTLENESS, KINDNESS, and unconditional LOVE! LORD, have MERCY. What a mighty GOD we serve. He does not let the ocean overflow the land no matter how the rivers run into it. Just think. He knew that I would write this and you would read it before He created the world. Can you see with the natural eye and then go further, seeing with the spiritual eye what kind of humungous, gigantic, mountainous GOD we serve? He is still bigger because He is everywhere at the same time. He is omnipresent. Have a blessed day, and remember GOD LOVES you, and so do I.

∼

## Day 95

Good morning, everyone! Today is GOD'S day! Let us rejoice and be glad - for our GOD is an awesome GOD. He's able to do way more than we can ask or think. Today PRAY for your soul to enter the kingdom of GOD. We need mighty warriors on the battlefield. Let's attack the enemy from every side - PRAY, PRAISE, WORSHIP, THANKSGIVING, and ADORATION to our KING JESUS CHRIST. Let us let the rain of these weapons flood HEAVEN - for our soul and the souls of those who do not know our ALMIGHTY GOD! Have a blessed day, and remember GOD LOVES you, and so do I.

## Day 96

Good morning, everyone! Today is GOD'S day! Let's shout for JOY! Let us kneel and WORSHIP our SAVIOR with humble submission this morning - for He alone is WORTHY of the PRAISE and WORSHIP. Let us leap for JOY this morning, shouting HALLELUJAH. He is WORTHY. He is WORTHY. JESUS is KING, JESUS is LORD. Our GOD will reign and rule forever. Let's PRAY for our loved ones. Let's keep them before the throne of our GOD as we plant seeds of RIGHTEOUSNESS. Have a blessed day, and remember GOD LOVES you, and so do I.

∼

## Day 97

Good morning, everyone! Today is GOD'S day! LORD, fill our cups this morning until they overflow, just pouring over to bless everyone we meet today. Prick their hearts, heal their hearts, and strengthen their hearts with the overflow. Let us JOYFULLY and CHEERFULLY share the overflow to bring GLORY to His name (JESUS, the SON of the LIVING GOD) - as we release the depression, trouble, etc. In others with the LOVE of GOD (word of GOD), we will be replenished by the power of GOD. Thank GOD for the refreshing. Can you feel it flooding our soul right now? Shout GLORY, HALLELUJAH! Have a blessed day, and remember GOD LOVES you, and so do I.

∼

## Day 98

Good morning, everyone! Today is GOD'S day! Let us PRAY in the SPIRIT until our hearts and souls have caught on fire, burning with the HOLY GHOST. Let us let the HOLY GHOST (SPIRIT) purge us so that we spread seeds of RIGHTEOUSNESS under all circumstances. So that our enemies will be overwhelmed and ask, "How do you live that type of life?" Our life is our witness. Let us PRAY until GOD rains down fire from HEAVEN consuming the sins of our soul. HALLELUJAH to the KING OF KINGS, our LORD and SAVIOR, JESUS CHRIST! Have a blessed day, and remember GOD LOVES you, and so do I.

## Day 99

Good morning, everyone! Today is GOD'S day! Let us plant the seed of servanthood. Through our pain, troubles, crises, heartache, etc., let us serve our MASTER (JESUS) by serving others. We will find that whatever we are going through will cease. We will get the VICTORY - for we are CHRIST-LIKE. JESUS served us with His life, death, and resurrection and now sits on the right hand of His father, interceding for us. So let us look beyond our feelings and emotions and get our blessings by serving cheerfully. Smile, and PRAISE our SAVIOR in the dance this morning. Have a blessed day, and remember GOD LOVES you, and so do I.

## Day 100

Good morning, everyone! Today is GOD'S day! Rise and shine, for the light has come to us - JESUS! Let us let Him shine in us brightly. Wrap those who don't know CHRIST with that seed of agape (unconditional LOVE). It is the LOVE that makes you cry. It makes you helpless and speechless. It makes you repent, crying, "LORD, forgive me." Let us nourish them. Have a blessed day, and remember GOD LOVES you, and so do I.

www.ingramcontent.com/pod-product-compliance
Lightning Source LLC
LaVergne TN
LVHW021403080426
835508LV00020B/2427